KILLING
YOURSELF
TO LIVE

A Journey From Darkness To Light

KILLING YOURSELF TO LIVE

A Journey From Darkness To Light

RANDY LEE RUBLE

ARPress
ILLUMINATING IDEAS.
EMPOWERING VOICES

ARPress
45 Dan Road Suite 5
Canton MA 02021
Hotline: 1(888) 821-0229
Fax: 1(508) 545-7580

Ordering Information:
Quantity sales. Special discounts are available on quantity purchases by corporations, associations, and others. For details, contact the publisher at the address above.

Printed in the United States of America.

ISBN-13:   Softcover   979-8-89356-406-8
           eBook   979-8-89356-405-1

Library of Congress Control Number: 2024902557

First, I would like to express my thankfulness to God; Without him none of this would be possible.

And I am grateful to the many people hub helped me in this process.

I would like to thank author William Henry, pastor Mike elder, pastor Robert may, pastor Rick cable, and pastor Paul Drake, for their support and guidance along the way. Also, pastor mark has, Sheila St Yan, Jan Aldridge, Dana clay, lane Hickman, and Harold Barlett (my Sunday school teacher when I was very young).

Last but not least, to my parents whom I put through a living hell for at least two decades. I hope they can finally say, "Praise God we're proud of you, son".

I am what I am but the grace of God. I am not ashamed of my life, my past is under the blood, never to be remembered by God anymore.

I want people to say do you remember how he was? Now look at him, I want to be like that. It takes as much grace to save a good person than it does a bad one.

- carl butch comma a good for nothing drunk as he said, turned evangelist.

CONTENTS

Introduction

Thanks be to God who has delivered me from all my addictions. It is only by his grace, and I am able to write this book.

My life has been a long, hard road to get me to the place where I am able to write this.

I have suffered many years of drug and alcohol abuse, three driving under the influence DUI's three overdoses many suicide attempts and mental ward admissions home confinement, substance abuse counseling, community service, probation, Alcoholics Anonymous, etc.- you name it, I've done it.

It is my great hope that the message of this journey will reach out and touch those who have gone down the same path I have traveled (or are heading that way) to reexamine their lives and turn it around before it's too late.

Because once you are dead, there is no turning back.

Chapter 1

The Good Years

The good years from the beginning of my life, I was raised in a good Christian home by loving parents.

In 1992, I graduated from high school with an A average and was always on the honor roll.

From junior high through high school, I was in the Boy Scouts of America and had earned more merit badges than anyone in the history of the troop, and earned the highest rank there is type in the Eagle Scout medal.

By 2006, I had joined the Civil Air Patrol with a second Lieutenant rank and could actually fly a Cessna airplane.

Little didn't know how much things would change but I turned 16 years old.

I will not dwell longer on the good years in this book, instead you will see the slippery slope, which is the main message I would like to present.

Chapter 2

The Beginning of sorrows

The beginning of sorrows but the time I was 16, I was driving, working at a restaurant, and thought I knew everything (like most teenagers).

No one ever told me I was going to get old, and I never really thought about it. My only philosophy was "Leave for the moment."

Sometimes I would tell my parents I had to work when in reality, mania where my days off. We will see where I was later on.

I would work over when other employees didn't show up for their shift, and it did that for one reason- the drugs and alcohol were there and available.

I was the youngest employee there so naturally I was very impressionable. Everyone who worked there was at least twice as old as me, so I was greatly influenced by the others whom I worked with.

Sadly, in my case, I became what I was surrounded by. I started drinking and doing drugs out of curiosity at first.

Eventually over the years, the fan of being curious had worn off. I had become both mentally and chemically dependent. And I would stoop to any level to get money.

I would lie; cheat; Steal from my parents, the waitresses, my friends, whoever; Never thinking of the past it would lead me down years later period but it was all part of God's plan.

Very often, someone would call off work at the last minute, and I would be asked to take their shift; So sometimes I was there from 9 in the morning to 1 at night. But the money was good and the place had its perks.

Several of the workers there were drug dealers who sold out of the bag type in door (like me) two others looking for drugs. And somewhere not small time dealers. I am talking about gun hypen packing once, and nearly all of them word ranks as well.

Nearly everyone in the kitchen was always "crooked." We all had those service station mugs that you couldn't see through, and we would help ourselves to the booze. There was a wide selection to choose from: a 55 gallon trash can on wheels full of Margarita mix (a vodka mixed drink).

We had dozens of different beers to choose from and to walk in the cooler.

Plus, there was plenty of whiskey of all kinds in the back of the store. It was behind a screen- in, locked cabinet but it was easy to get into when you can pick locks and are surrounded by criminals eager to teach you things and share information. It was a very successful restaurant somehow; If they only knew who the kitchen crew was cooking their food.

Plus, we would always go outside to the dumpster to smoke dope. It was closed and with a wooden fence so jumping and dumps there was perfect place to hide.

Now to me this place was great, I worked there for eight years from the time I was 16 to 24. I was eventually fired supposedly for slamming someone up against the wall, with a steak knife to their throat wanting to see what color their blood was. I remember none of it.

During these years I discovered music, all the 1960s psychedelic era, which went great with drugs and booze. What more could a long-haired hippie want out of life?

I discovered concerts beautiful live music. And these years, I saw the Grateful Dead many times, which was a big party on wheels. It traveled from city to city partying.

And I have so many more bands like ACDC, The Moody Blues The Allman Brothers. Lynyrd Skynyrd karma Nirvana, tool, Alice in Chains, Pink Floyd, rush, Roger waters, and more hypen I just wish I could remember more of it. Most of the time was a blackout to me. I discovered LSD (a very powerful hallucinogenic drug), and I was afraid of nothing when it comes to partying. I remember seeing the Grateful Dead on 1994 in Ohio at Buckeye Lake. I took ten hits of acid and walked down the hill to the show. I found out 20 years later when new tube while watching the show, that the rain poured down for hours.

I never noticed it at the time period most of the chapters in my life is a blur to me. I am prone to blackouts, so when I would go to a concert or party, I can't really remember much, which is a pretty scary thought when you are driving hundreds of miles to a show and can only remember bits and pieces. I have awaken in different states not knowing how I've got there. They come out with a drink cold 4 loco once (which is illegal now in its original form). It was alcohol and caffeine mixed, which would put you in a wide awake, walking, talking, drunk blackout.

I saw it and bought eight of them at a gas station, never realizing what it truly was; I just assumed it was a new beer.

I woke up the next day down by the flood wall by a river with no idea how I had gotten there nor why didn't the night before. This was my life back then I was very self-centered and selfish, thinking that the whole world revolved around me. My whole life was partying and music. Like I said earlier, little didn't know the path of misery it would take me down. I couldn't see it. My choices were all part of God's plan; in his mercy, Jesus will mold us and shape our lives in spite of the choices we make. It's a matter of free will. The evil can only do what God allows him to do in our lives, and he can go no further.

I was writing the devils coattails, being ripped apart from the inside out without even realizing it. It was like God and the devil playing ping pong with my life, basically bearing me half to death for many many years I think I must have a skull about 3 inches thick because nothing could get in, and I had a head like a hole, any advice went in one ear and out the other period but if I had to play this deadly game and go through everything in my life that I've been through not to split hell wide open, it was all worth it. I would not be able to write this story of an imaginable truth and desperation without a test.

Chapter 3

The Night Life of Darkness

The night life of darkness while I was still working at the restaurant, I was drinking in bars at the age of 16 as well. One bar and I adopted as my favorite because a co-worker lived right down the road from it. We usually work together, so when we ended our ships at work being drunk, off the bar we would go.

There was a big confederate flag in each of the front window so none could see in. It was a "redneck" bar and a very rough place.

But I was accepted there by then. I was defining hippie kid. I play David Allen Coe on the jukebox for hours over and over. His songs fit the place well. Some of the people are sitting there right this minute just like when I was a kid. Sadly, a lot of the old timers I had met years ago home I loved like brothers have died. I still think of many of them. They are not bad people, they were just last, making bad choices as I did.

And it's a vicious cycle that will repeat over and over in your life if you let it. I did.

There was a big sign on the wall of the bar that stated "We don't call 911," and that was the truth. If you were a stranger looking for trouble, you just found it. Once, a man was shot in there through the window (thus the reason for bullet proof glass to be installed afterwards).

The round heat the pool table, bounce off, and hit him right in the lever. Sadly, I was there and saw this unfold before my eyes. He was my friend, just sitting in the wrong spot at that time unfortunately.

He was carried out by the medics that night, but he never stopped drinking. Years later, because of that night's event, his liver was failing. The last time I ever saw him, he was all swollen up and turning yellow from jaundice. He died away; The way we all lived.

The bartender was always drunk, which never helped matters any period I used to get off work and then off to the bar, and I'd stay until the supposed closing time at 2:00 in the morning and help him clean, mob, and take out trash. His dead now too, along with many others I had come to know so well over the years.

Sometimes we would just turn out the lights come on lock the doors, and play poker for hours, a lot of the time until the sun was coming up. But the place was just like my job, no one ever wanted to leave. All the drugs you could ever want was there. There was no last call for alcohol and if you want it out you would just leave out the back door. They used to try and take my keys because I was pretty crazy and it didn't care about anything but myself. If someone did manage to get them, I always had another key in my wallet or car anyways because I was always sneaky, or so I thought.

This is the reason I have DUIs, all from the same bar.

I stated earlier that sometimes I would tell my parents I had to work on my days off, but I would be at the bar. Drinking and driving was always fun for me. Thanks be to God I never killed anyone during the drive home because of my stupidity. One of my friends from there did hit someone head on and killed one person and crippled the passenger for life. He's still in prison to this day. All of this was in between me being 16 and 24 years old. I had seen and done a lot of crazy things by Dan, but that was just the beginning of sorrows for me.

Chapter 4

What you do affects others.

I am very sorry my parents had to see all of this happened to me up to this point in my life at age 24. They basically had to go through it as an outsider on the sidelines. But I know they were always praying for me, along with many others. By this time, I had built a wall around my mind. Just like in Pink Floyd, the wall, and no one could get in, I couldn't get out either.

Drinking and doing drugs is very selfish, self-centered sport, and I was just captain of the All Star team. It affects everyone around you, both directly and indirectly. Your actions, your words, what others tell them about you, but you can't see it. I was always a nice person until I started drinking, then you turn into something completely different once your mind, judgment, and reasoning are impaired. I've been told by many I was like two different people, almost like a person with split personality disorder. You never knew what one of me would show up, and I could turn into the other me in no time flat with booze and drugs. The devil has put blinders on your eyes, and you are completely unaware as to how bad of the state of mind and shape you are really in, both mentally and physically. You cannot realize what they see you have become. I remember looking at my parents and saying, I don't want anything to do with you or your God. Their hearts were broken by me saying that, and I would go on to regret those words, but God's plan was not done.

Chapter 5

Wisdom.

God knows that we are going to do before we do it, even before we are born. Jeremiah one verse 5 says, before I formed the in the belly, I musee. So, if he knew Jeremiah he knew all of us too. That's the good, the bud, everything, for all of us. All that you are ever going to do in life he already knows. This does that mean that our lives are on a priest in path that has been predetermined. We have free will, a choice. We all have a choice in life for everything one path leads you down one way. Another choice leads your life in another direction, just like in the Led Zeppelin lyrics to stairway to heaven. There are two pads that you can go by / but in the long run there's still time to change the road you're on. These words ring very true, you can change paths but it's a long way to get back. I used to blame God for everything. Why is this happening to me over and over? why am I in jail again? why am I in the psych ward again? why won't you just let me die?" one answer: wrong road-but choices define my destiny, and was all part of his plan of shaping me into what I am today.

Chapter 6

I knew it all.

I stated earlier that I graduated from high school in 1992 with an "A" average, was always on the honor roll, and I don't think I ever took a tix book home. Like most kids at age 18, you couldn't tell me anything. I knew it all, or so I thought. I was still working at the restaurant at this time period once, I was driving my car down the road right in front all of it after a party. I still had some Yukon Jack whiskey left in the litter, and I took a bunch of valium (blue 10mg ones) and if it rained too. They were little pink heart-shaped feels you could buy at any gas station back then. It was speed. They are illegal now since ephedrine is one of the ingredients in crystal meth um feta mean. Well, I thought, I'm going to kill myself now since I feel the world would be better off without me and warped mine. Years of chemical abuse had led me to severe depression. So I was driving very fast and decided to hit a telephone pole head right in front of where I worked. I hate it alright, cut it in half like hot butter and push it down the road and cracked another one period how bad did I get hurt? I didn't. I was wearing no seat belt, but drugs and dope heads are very bouncy. I hit my face on the steering wheel and had a cut on my chin under my lip. That's all. there were electric wires arcing all around, several of them right outside my car. I heard someone yell don't get out you'll get electrocuted I'm not sure if it was the police medics coworkers or strangers. I had no idea. I yelled back out the window you don't understand, electricity can't kill me!" well I got the idea from I'm not sure, but I was their man possessed at this time in my life and insane, since the definition of insanity is doing the same thing over and over, only to achieve the same results. I get out of the car, walked to the ambulance on my own, and best out. They couldn't even give me a DUI because they couldn't wake me up. I can barely remember waking up in the hospital, but the first thing I remember seeing was my dad, who was always there for me, no matter what I did. I wish I could say the same, but sadly, I can't.

Chapter 7

Screwed blued and tattooed.

Once, I was severely beaten with an inch of my life in a bar fight. (where, I don't ever know.) I look like I fell off a mountain, I was black, purple, red, blue. Naturally, the police last the pictures they took, so they were never seen in court for it. But what about the two guys who did it? One ended up dead outside of a bar burned up in his car. They said he passed out and dropped a cigarette, but I don't believe that. I figure someone killed him. The other one is in prison for murder, many years after the first one died. And these were friends of mine period to this day, I have no idea what we were fighting about. They threw me out of the car right in front of the old man's house who owned the bar I always went to. The old man saved my life that day. He's gone now too, but I'll never forget him as long as I leave. I've been literally dragged out of my house by the police when I've come home drunk as a skunk. Once, my father and I got in a fight when I was like this, and I cracked him in the head with a huge for but battery mag flashlight when his back was turned. Some son I had become.

They took me away that night, and I was screaming about the demons. God was trying to get my attention. I've tried to kill myself more times and ways than I care to remember.

Once I tried to hang myself upstairs at home, the rope broke. I've slit my wrists before. I've overdosed and had my stomach pumped with activated charcoal. It's the same stuff used in fish tank filters but in liquid form, and it's really nasty.

I've been thrown in the psychiatric ward more than once. If you think you are crazy, go there. You'll find out that you are not half as bad off as some of those tortured souls.

However, none of this opened my eyes at all. One time, they were going to send me off somewhere in Ohio to a mental institution for a six- week evaluation after I slit my wrists. I can remember a woman at the hospital asking me, "Who's going to pay for all of this?" I told her I guess she was since it was her idea because I sure wasn't. They sent me home that day.

Chapter 8

Truth Hurts

In Mathew 4:7, it says, "Thou shall not tempt thy lord thy God." I had gone well beyond that point by now.

This was in 1996, and I planned on being dead by the time I was twenty- seven, just like Jim Morrison, Janis Joplin, and Jimi Hendrix- who all died at twenty- seven years old. I was on the highway to hell, on a crazy train with no brakes on, and I did not care.

Chapter 9

Happy New Year, You're Under Arrest

On January 1st, 1997, I had the "pleasure" of being the first person arrested in my country DUI. I asked the cop if I would get medal for it. Not being amused, he gave me a pair of metal bracelets instead. I was originally sentenced to six months of home confinement for that one. I made it a whole two weeks until I decided to get good and drunk, so home confinement was a failure for me, so off to jail I went. I did four and a half months in jail for that one. Not once did one of my supposed friends ever visit me or c all even once, they were too busy doing the things we always did --- get wasted. They forgot about me, but God didn't. When I was released, the first place I went to was the drug dealer's house, the second was the bar.

My last one was in 2007, ten years after, same road, almost in the same spot. For some reason, three of my DUI were there except one they were so close to my house. I could have walked from where I was pulled over. This last DUI they were going to send me to prison for a year or more.

Thankfully, after hiring a five-thousand-dollar lawyer for five minutes of work, they settled on home confinement.

Lynn Hickman and Dana Clay (two people from the church my parents were attending) came to see me while I was in jail for the 1997 DUI.

It was a noble gesture by my parents who would do anything in the world for me, but you cannot ride your parent's coattails into Heaven no matter how much they want you to change.

You have to want to change.

You have to have a heart connection with Jesus, not just to go through the motions to please your parents and get them off your back. You can know the Bible forwards, backwards, and upside down, and have the brain connection, but it will come to no avail unless you have the heart connection, a personal relationship with Jesus Christ.

It took me a long time to figure that out because I was just going through the motions.

Maybe someone reading this book will figure it out way before I did. Just writing this all down makes me want to cry seeing how selfish I was.

But I was in pain, all self- inflicted.

Chapter 10

Darkness- Grey- Light

In 1998, I finally rededicated my life to Jesus after talking to Dana Clay. He was a preacher who used to be like me and had been a member of the Pagan Motorcycle gang, someone I could relate to.

But just because you are saved by the blood of Jesus does not mean that the devil is going to leave you alone. To the contrary, that is when he's going to throw everything, he got at you. He will start fighting you a thousand times harder than before. He had you once, there is no need to battle for your soul.

When you get saved, he will come after you, full force, to tempt you to mess up and go back to your old ways, so that you will just give up and give in.

That is where I was right then, encircled on all sides. Just because you are saved does not mean that you're not going to fall flat on your face and mess everything up. All you can do is just get back up. Look at my life, it was like a toy yo-yo, going up and down repeatedly.

CHAPTER 11

Trying

In 1999, I used to travel all over the place in my state with preacher named Mark Hess, I would give my testimony, and he would preach. I was on fire for the Lord.

I've been on mission trips to Honduras, to El Sembrador, to a Christian boy's school way back in the jungle, and they do a great work.

It's a boys' school for the poor kids down there to get a Christ-centered education and learn about the Lord. It was very beautiful place, and I did not want to leave.

Those kids did not have much in life materially, but they were innocent, not corrupted by big city life, television, video games, etc.

There was none of those there. The place did well to keep their electric generator running. But they had an inner peace about them, something I longed for, that I needed for so long.

Up to this point, I had been searching for the truth at the cost of living.

Chapter 12

Killing Yourself To Live

From 1999 or so until 2017, I had been on the fire at times for God, cold, the lukewarm. Everything for me just ran in a circle of pain, and I had managed to get myself back into drinking and drugs again.

At the end of April of 2017, I flew to Las Vegas, Nevada- the "city of lights" surrounded by complete darkness. You can see this if you are flying in the at night. There is nothing else around it. I went and was there for two weeks, fully planning on never coming back alive.

The events leading up to this trip started with my father having diverticulitis surgery in November 2016. They cut two or three feet of his intestines out, a very serious surgery.

They told mom and I at the hospital that there would be in home health care available for him, and they would be there to help us. That was very little encouragement and little help from these agencies.

He was on intravenous food for ninety days, no food by mouth. Basically, the home health people who were supposed to be so much help was a lie. They came and taught us and expected the family to do it. So I had to learn how to change the IV food bags daily, mix drugs they sent in vials to shoot in the IV bags, program an electronic pump that runs all this stuff. Then connect the tubes to the pump, then connect the tubes to the pump, then to the bag, then into a pick line in his arm. And all this had to be done sterile and very carefully so he would not get any infection.

My mother had to dress the foot long wound daily throughout all of this. What we didn't knowing is the doctor left a hole in his intestines. So just when he seemed to be doing okay, back to the hospital he would go.

We all went through an extremely difficult time with this from November until May 2016 daily. Plus, my father and I had never gotten along very well to begin with in those many years, since it's been previously written, I could not be trusted. We get along much better now.

If they were gone for twenty minutes in previous years, I could be up the road and back with cases of beer, wine, whiskey, pretty much everything.

My dad and my personalities are too much alike whether he wants to admit it or not. Where most are very stubborn people.

He was in and out of the hospital five times during all of this. So after months of almost losing him, I felt very overwhelmed for five months of very nervous nurse. But even he's the surgery was in God's plan. I took off after being under so much stress from this, I had all I could take and just snapped. Going out the front door with no shoes on, nothing but the clothes when my back and my wallet. I told no one goodbye or anything. I figured they would find out what happened to their worthless good for nothing son on the news of the computer. I had it all figured out or so it seemed, but God had other plans. This was my life in Las Vegas. God let the devil put an idea in my head to go to Las Vegas for a reason, but I did not know this until later. my parents have never ever heard any of this party of my story period but i know there is someone out there in the world who will read this book and can entirely relate to this history. You might be in Topeka, Kansas, maybe 4th Lauderdale, Florida; maybe someone in Italy, Spain, or Russia.

God knows exactly where you are and who this is for. It is my hope that you will be touched and forever be changed by the story to come. It doesn't matter to me how much shame I bring upon myself for all of this. This is the battle for my soul and yours. My plan was a simple one to die, I planned on jumping off the top of a casino and smashed face first into a car the casino was giving away, which is always parked there by the free month St entrance. They give one away every few days or week. I've been to Las Vegas twice, and there is always a car park there and I have never seen it without one period what a better and feeling end to a failed life for a loser then to do a face plant 30 stories off the roof straight down into spotless car that would retail for hundreds of thousands of dollars period that was the plan god had a better one.

CHAPTER 13

The Seven Miracles In Vegas

Miracle #1 after a few days of relaxing and partying, looking at all the thousands of lights from my room, I made my way to the roof planning to smash that car. I looked over the edge, and the car was gone. God moved that car!

It was in his plan, all of this, everything in my life had led me here. But I was far from done because when I messed something up, I go all out.

So I made my way back down to the crowds and the thousands of other lost souls on Fremont Street. Cars are not allowed down there, it's strictly for pedestrian only four blocks.

Miracle #2 I smoke crack for three days straight with a guy from my state, that is 72 hours of no sleep, no food, just cracked, weed, whiskey, beer, pills. That should have been enough to kill us both.

Miracle #3 after this, I tried for days to drink myself to death. I didn't even get sick from all the dope and booze in the toll two weeks.

Miracle #4 by this time on the trip, I was getting pretty aggravated with the whole situation. So I bought 4/5 of fireball whiskey and acquired 20 more Finn pain pills. I figure this should do it. I just drank and do it all, lay back in my room, and never wake up again. Nope.

The next morning I woke up in my fancy casino room completely sober.

Miracle #5 now I was in that room for a week before this, and I looked all over the place in there for anything someone might have hidden, lost, or stashed in a hurry. I also noted in my mind there was not a Gideon Bible in that room, like others I had been and previously on this trip. But when I woke up after the 20 morphine pills and four bottles of whiskey, on my bed was a Gideon Bible opened to one Corinthians 10 verse 13, and it was highlighted in yellow, nothing else was highlighted or marked in the entire book. There has no temptation taken you but such as in common to man; but God is faithful, who will not suffer you to be tempted above that ye are able; but will with the temptation also make way to escape, that ye may be able to bear with. (Corinthians 10:13)

Miracle #6 then I remembered my room key card and the number on it. It was room number 1013!

Miracle #7 I am alive and forever changed the devil played upon all my weaknesses and tried everything to kill me, and God would not allow it to happen. He only has so much power over man that God allows him. Now I've had miracles happen in my life, but seven at once? I knew this way my sign from God. I thought to myself, I gave up, there's no reason in even trying anymore. God still had a purpose for my life. So I stayed in that room for three more days, reading the Gideon Bible God had put at the side of my bed. I had no intention of leaving in Las Vegas for two weeks. After all this, I did manage to get bronchitis though. I wanted to call home, but I figured everyone would just tell me to stay there. So I summed up the courage I could muster within me to call home, and I talked to my mom, never mentioning any of the miracles that had happened to me in Sin City to her, except that it was and seasonably cold there, and I was getting pretty sick coughing my head off. It was three in the morning back home, and she asked me if I knew how long I had been gone. I guess three to four days because I had no idea really, I didn't even have a watch with me. She told me I had been gone for two weeks! seemed like a few days to me. Las Vegas never closes, so there is really not a time there but day and night to tourist. I had to get out of there but I felt the need to go to the Las Vegas rescue mission first. I checked out of the casino, which was pretty easy since I'm a light traveler with only the clothes on my back.

So I went to the mission. They were having a service, so I sat down and listened to the speaker while I waited to talk to the head of the mission. I told him everything I have written here about my experience, and he told me, "Son, you get a second chance and take it and get out of Vegas while I still could."

I told him it was about my hundredth chance, and I was going to the airport. Getting to Las Vegas is easy, but getting out is much harder. I finally found a flight after trying a dozen or more different airlines. The only one I could get was eight hours away. If I had to wait eight hours, OK. I just wanted out. After walking for what seemed like miles, I found my gate and just waited forever. The airport out there is humongous, it's bigger than my whole town.

CHAPTER 14

Modern Day Sodom And Gomorrah

There is so much pain and suffering in Las Vegas that you never hear about. All that you see on TV is the lights.

It is the modern-day Sodom and Gomorrah in every way. People go out there with aspirations of hitting it big and loose everything, including their lives.

Someone just came up behind a guy and hit him in the temple for no reason, and he dropped dead on the sidewalk. I was 15 foot away and witness this. That could have easily been me laying there the street of Las Vegas are full of beggars, St performers, musicians drug dealers, prostitutes, con artist, drunks and dope heads.

In casino bathrooms, on more than one occasion, I saw hypodermic needles from people shooting up sitting in the stalls, it would not be a good place to be a janitor to say the least.

And that is just above ground there is an underground Vegas too, the one you never hear anything about. There are thousands of people who use indoctrination tunnels under the bright lights of the city streets. These are rivers (more like concrete creeks) that are huge underground tunnel systems that go for miles for water drainage, and they are full of people who dreamed big and lost it all, or gambling all their money away or their addictions placed them there.

There's a song by Colin ray called "What if Jesus came back like that?"

Like a hobo under a bridge and hooked on crack, would you let him in or turn your back?

What if Jesus come back like that? it's a very sad song. His stop and think for a minute come on now what if Jesus come back like that? who did Jesus come to save? the lost. he hung out with the dregs of society and South them out, or they sought him out. The lame, the beggars, prostitutes, drunks, thieves, the demon possessed. The forgotten ones that society has always looked down upon, in modern times and His.

He didn't hang out with the Pharisees and Sadducees, who were the "holier than these people of His day. It's just like that today, nothing has changed.

It's just like the Ray Stephens song "The Mississippi Squirrel Revival," which says "Way down on the amen pew / sat Mrs. Bertha better than you."

Nobody is better than me and I'm certainly no better than anyone else, we are all the same. A beggar is not better or worse than a Wall Street broker in God's eyes. He looks at your heart, now what you are wearing the beggar could be a Christian, and a guy in the suit lost on his way to hell. Appearances can be deceiving as we are very judgmental people.

I don't care if you have $10 million in the bank, drive a porch, and have a diamond ring that weighs a pound. That does not impress me in the least, and it certainly does not impress God. What is in your heart does, not material things.

Chapter 15

You Can Run, But You Can't Hide

Hebrews 13 verse 2, be not forgetful to entertain strangers, for this some have entertained angels unaware very true, I have had the hand of God upon me my whole life, even when I did not want it or realize it. Angels were all around me in spite of myself. I can't kill myself, nor do I have any desire to do so anymore.

The miracles in Las Vegas taught me that because Jesus had a purpose for my life throughout all of this, the devil has lost me for good. There's no turning back for me now. To what? my purpose in sharing all of this is to reach those who are deemed hopeless. No one is beyond God's reach, including the drunks, dopers, junkies, the ones who have traveled the road I did. There is hope, if you have never walked where I have been, you can talk to people like me and tell you are blue in the face, and still you will never get through. They need someone to relate to, I needed someone to relate to. We all do.

I hope those reading this can relate to my story. It doesn't matter how far down you have fallen. Never give up on yourself!

I've hit rock bottom so many times (I've thought), only to fall farther. All my life I have been tested (and failed) over and over for a purpose.

I've always knew God had a calling on my life for something special. I could end up like Paul and become what I most despised.

Maybe it was the right test period but there was always a calling that I felt, I just always chose to run from it. No matter how strong or how you get, you can't hide from God and you can't hide from yourself either no one tried many others have, it never works.

CHAPTER 16

Tired

A s a man thinketh in his heart, so is he.

---Proverbs 23:7

I wonder how many people out there feeling so alone, depressed, without hope, worthless, with no one to even talk to? That's how I felt also. I'm tired of running. I've spent hundreds of thousands of dollars running from myself and God to finally realize this: I've been my own worst enemy my entire life. I've spent my life seeking all that was still unsaid. Now I am saying it. Someone will read these words and understand because they are going through it.

If I can reach one soul that's on the same path I was, it was worth it all. People always say " if I could only go back and change this or that in my life," in some cases this can be true to some people. In my case, it is not. I would not change a thing.

Are you my story is who I am, and I am my story. You can't have a testimony without a test, I just hope and pray yours doesn't take along as mine. I am leaving to submit that God can use the devil to open your eyes, if you can survive it. Don't be like me and waste half your life looking for the obvious, it was always right in front of my face. I've done nearly every drug mankind has ever invented (enough to fill warehouse). it's a miracle I have any brains left. But they can never fill the void in your heart like Jesus can.

CHAPTER 17

The Sound Of Silence
A Song By Simon And Garfunkel

Fools I said you do not know,

Silence like a cancer grows.

Hear my words that I might teach you.

Take my arms that I might reach you.

But my words like silent raindrops fell.

And echoed in the wells of silence.

And the people bowed and prayed.

To the neon gods they made.

And design flushed out its final warning,

and the words that it was forming.

And the sign said the words of the prophets are written on the subway walls,

and tenement halls and whispered in the sounds of silence.

People writing songs that voices never share,

and no one dare disturb the sound of silence.

The point: please do not do what I have done in this book. If you have mental or substance abuse issues, don't be silent like I chose to be and shut everyone out. Silence will try its best to kill you.

CHAPTER 18

God's Simple Plan Of Salvation

I am asking you the most important question of your life. Your joy and eternity depend upon your answer. The question is: are you saved? it's not a question of how good you are or if you go to church, but "are you saved?" Are you sure you will go to heaven when you die?

Jesus can deliver you from all your addictions and the road you are on, just like me. There is no one so bad or nothing you have done that you cannot be saved. There is no unpardonable sin.

First, you need to realize that you are a Sinner. Because you are a Sinner, you are condemned to death. This includes eternal separation from God in hell. But God loves us so much (even when we do not want or deserve it), that he gave his son Jesus to bear our sins and die in our place. Jesus had to shed his blood and die.

Although we cannot understand how, God said my sins and your scenes were laid upon Jesus on the cross and he died in our place. He became our substitute; this is true---God cannot lie.

"For whosoever shall call upon the name of the Lord shall be saved" (romance 10: 13). whosoever includes me and you, all, no matter how drunk or high you are. Jesus said, "Come as you are."

If you are like me and have to learn everything the hard way through substance abuse, suicide attempts, jails, then you know in your heart you are a Sinner. Right now, wherever you are, possibly someplace you know in your heart you shouldn't be, lift your heart to heaven and prayer. Just pray, "God, I knew I am a senior, I believe Jesus was my substitute when he died on the cross. He shared his blood, died, was buried, and was resurrected for me. I now receive him as my savior. I thank you for the forgiveness of my sins, and the gift of salvation and everlasting life. Amen."

Remember, your soul is worth more than all the world. If it was only you and earth, Jesus still would have come and given his life for you.

CHAPTER 19

Bible Verses About Salvation

Ye must be born again. (John 3:7)

For all have sinned and come short of the glory of God. (Romans 3.23)

For the wages of sin is death, but the gift of God is eternal life through Jesus Christ our Lord. (Romans 6:23)

It's appointed unto men once to die, but after this the judgement. (Hebrew 9:27)

God commandeth all men everywhere to repent. (Acts 17:30)

Sirs, what most I do be saved, and they said Believe on the Lord Jesus Christ, and thou shall be saved and thy house. (Acts 16:30)

For God so loved the world, that he sent his only begotten Son, that who so ever believeth in him shall not perish but have everlasting life. (John 3:16)

For whosoever shall call upon the name of the Lord shall be saved. (Romans 10:13)

CHAPTER 20

Bible Verses About Drugs, Alcohol And Demons

Revelation 18 verse 23, "and the light of a condo show shine no more at all in thee, and the voice of the bridegroom and of the bride shall be heard no more at all in thee: for thy merchants were the great men of the earth; for by thy sorceries were all nations deceived." now sorceress are magical arts, positions, and poisons. For this, we derived the English word pharmacies, from the Greek word pharmakeia signified the use of medicine, drugs, spells, then poisoning, then witchcraft. Taken from the Greek Dictionary of the New Testament in Strong's *Concordance* by James Strong (1890).

Who hath woe? Who hath sorrow? Who hath contentions? Who hath babbling? Who hath wounds without cause? Who hath redness of the eyes?

They that tarry long at the wine; they that go to seek mixed wine.

Look not thou upon the wine when it is red, when it giveth his color in the cup, when it moveth itself aright.

At last it biteth like a serpent, and stingeth like an adder.

Thine eyes shall behold strange women, and thine heart shall utter perverse things.

Yea thou shalt be as he that lieth down in the midst of the sea, or as he that lieth upon the top of a mast.

They have sticken me, shalt thou say, and I was not sick; They have beaten me and I felt it not; when shall I awake? I will seek it yet again. (Proverbs 23:29-35)

Let us walk honestly, as in the day, not in a rioting and drunkenness, not in chambering and wantonness, not in strife and envying. (Romans 13:13)

Wine is a mocker; strong drink is raging and whosoever is deceived thereby is not wise. (Proverbs 20:1)

For they that sleep, sleep in the night and they that be drunken are drunken in the night.

But let us, who are of the day, be sober, putting on the breast plate of faith and love, and for a helmet, the hope of salvation.

The separation of day and night and the drunk at night in the Bible. (I Thessolonians 5:7-8)

Ironic, I titled a Journey from Darkness to Light and never noticed this.

DEMONS

The Demoniac Boy Cured

And when he came to his disciples, he saw a great multitude about them, and the scribes questioning with them.

And straightway all the people when they beheld ham, we greatly amazed, and ran into him saluted him.

And he asked the scribes, what question ye with them?

And one of the multitude answered and said, master, I have brought unto thee my son, which has a dumb spirit;

and wheresoever he taketh him, he teareth him: and he foameth, and gnasheth with his teeth, and pineth away: and I spake to thy disciples that they should cast him out; and they could not.

He answereth him, and saith, O faithless generation, how long shall I suffer you? Bring him unto me.

And they brought him unto him: and when he saw him, straightway the spirit tare him; and he fell on the ground, and wallowed foaming.

And he asked his father, How long is it ago since this came unto him? And he said, Of a child.

And oft times it hath cast him into the fire, and into the waters, to destroy him: but if thou canst do anything, have compassion on us, and help us.

Jesus sain unto him, If thou canst believe, all things are possible to him that believeth.

And straightway the father of the child cried out, and said with tears, Lord, I believe; help thou mine unbelief.

When Jesus saw that the people came running together, he rebuked the foul spirit, saying unto him,

Thou dumb and deaf spirit, I charge thee, come out of him, and enter no more into him.

And the spirit cried, and rent him sore, and came out of him: and he was as one dead; insomuch that many said, He is dead.

But Jesus took him by the hand, and lifted him up; and he arose.

And when he was come into the house, his disciples asked him privately, Why could not we cast him out?

And he said unto them, This kind can come forth by nothing, but by prayer and fasting. (Mark 9:14-29)

Madman of Gadara

And they came over unto the other side of the sea, into the country of the Gadarenes.

And when he was come out of the ship, immediate they met him out of the tombs a man with an unclean spirit,

Who had his dwelling among the tombs; and nom an could bind him, no, not with chains:

Because that he had been often bound with fetters and chains, and the chains had been plucked asunder by him, and the fetters broken in pieces: neither could any man tame him.

And always, night and day, he was in the mountains, and in the tombs, crying, and cutting himself with stones.

But when he saw Jesus afar off, he ran and worshipped him,

And cried with a loud voice, and said, What have I to do with thee, Jesus, thou Son of the most high God? I adjure thee by God, that thou torment me not.

For he said unto him, Come out of the man, thou unclean spirit.

And he asked him, What is thy name? And he answered, saying, My name is Legion: for we are many.

And he besought him much that he would not send them away out of the country.

Now there was there nigh unto the mountains a great herd of swine feeding.

And all the devils besought him, saying, Send us into the swine, that we may enter into them.

And forthwith Jesus gave them leave. And the unclean spirits went out, and entered into the swine: and the herd ran violently down a steep place into the sea, (they were about two thousand;) and were choked in the sea.

And they that fed the swine fled, and told it in the city, and in the country. And they went out to see what it was that was done.

And they come to Jesus, and see him that was possessed with the devil, and had the legion, sitting, and clothed, and in his right mind: and they were afraid.

And they that saw it told them how it befell to him that was possessed with the devil, and also concerning the swine.

And they began to pray him to depart out of their coasts.

And when he was come into the ship, he that had been possessed with the devil prayed him that he might be with him.

Howbeit Jesus suffered him not, but saith unto him, Go home to thy friends, and tell them how great things the Lord hath done for thee, and hath had compassion on thee.

And he departed, and began to publish in Decapolis how great things Jesus had done for him: and all men did marvel. (Mark 5:1-20)

And they arrived at the country of the Gadarenes, which is over against Galilee. And when he went forth to land, there met him out of the city a certain man, which had devils ling time, and ware no clothes, neither abode in any house, but in the tombs,

When he saw Jesus, he cried out, and fell down before him, and with a loud voice said, what have I to do with thee, Jesus, thou Son of God most high? I beseech thee, torment me not.

(For he had commanded the unclean spirit to come out of the man. For oftentimes it had caught him: and he was kept bound with chains and in fetters; and he brake the bands, and was driven of t he devil into the wilderness.)

And Jesus asked him, saying, What is thy name? And he said, Legion: because many devils were entered into him.

And the besought him that he would not command them to go out into the deep.

And there was there a herd of many swine feeding on the mountain: and they besought him that he would suffer them to enter into the. And he suffered them.

Then went the devils out of the man, and entered into the swine: and the herd ran violently down a steep place into the lake, and were choked.

When they that fed them saw what was done, they fled, and went and told it in the city and in the country.

Then they went out to see what was done; and came to Jesus, and found the man, out of whom the devils were departed, sitting at the feet of Jesus, clothed, and in his right mind: and they were afraid.

They also which saw it told them by what means he that was possessed of the devils was healed.

Then the whole multitude of the country of the Gadarenes roundabout besought him to depart from them; for they were taken with great fear: and he went up into the ship, and returned back again.

Now the man out of whom the devils were departed besought him that he might be with him: but Jesus sent him away, saying, Return to thine own house, and shew how great things God hath dine unto thee. And he went his way, and published throughout the whole city how great things Jesus had done unto him.

And it came to pass, that, when Jesus was returned, the people gladly received him: for they were all waiting for him. (Luke 8:26-40)

NOTES

NOTES

NOTES

NOTES

NOTES

NOTES

NOTES

NOTES

NOTES

NOTES

NOTES

NOTES

NOTES

NOTES

NOTES

NOTES

NOTES

NOTES

NOTES

NOTES